contents

roll-up baby blanket

Yarn 4

Vanna's Choice by Lion Brand Yarn Co., 3½oz/100g skeins, each approx 170yd/156m (acrylic)
• 3 skeins Soft Pink #103(A)

Vanna's Choice Baby by Lion Brand Yarn Co., 3½oz/100g skeins, each approx 170yd/155m (acrylic)
• 2 skeins Sweet Pea #169 (B)

Hook

Size J/10 (6mm) crochet hook OR SIZE NEEDED TO OBTAIN GAUGE

Additional

• Tapestry needle

Measurements

32"/81cm x 32"/81cm

Gauge

11 sts and 9 rows to 4" (10cm) over patt st
TAKE TIME TO CHECK YOUR GAUGE

Note

Ch-3 counts as 1 dc throughout.

Blanket

With A, ch 69.
Row 1 (RS) Sc in 4th ch from hook (beg-ch counts as 1 dc), dc in next ch, *sc in next ch, dc in next ch. Rep from * across. Ch 1, turn—67 sts.
Row 2 Sc in 1st dc, *dc in next sc, sc in next dc. Rep from * across. Ch 3, turn.
Row 3 *Sc in next dc, dc in next sc. Rep from * across. Ch 1, turn.
Rep Rows 2 & 3 for pattern until piece measures 24" (61 cm) from beg. Fasten off.

Finishing
Border

Rnd 1 With RS facing, join B with sl st in any corner of Blanket, ch 1, 3 sc in corner, *work 67 sc evenly spaced across edge of Blanket to next corner, 3 sc in next corner; rep from * twice, work 67 sc evenly spaced across last edge of Blanket, join rnd with sl st in 1st sc—280 sc.
Rnd 2 Ch 1, sc in same st as sl st, (dc, sc, dc) in next sc (corner made), *sc in next sc, (dc in next sc, sc in next sc) 34 times, (dc, sc, dc) in next sc (corner made). Rep from * twice, (sc in next sc, dc in next sc) to end of rnd, join rnd with sl st in 1st sc—288 sts.
Rnd 3 Ch 3, sc in next dc, (dc, sc, dc) in next sc (corner made), *sc in next dc, (dc in next sc, sc in next dc) 35 times, (dc, sc, dc) in next sc (corner made).Rep from * twice, sc in next dc, (dc in next sc, sc in next dc) to end of rnd, join rnd with sl st in top of beg-ch—296 sts.
Rnd 4 Ch 1, sc in same st as sl st, dc in next sc, sc in next dc, (dc, sc, dc) in next sc (corner made), *sc in next dc, (dc in next sc, sc in next dc) 36 times, (dc, sc, dc) in next sc (corner made). Rep from * twice, (sc in next dc, dc in next sc) to end of rnd; join with sl st in 1st sc—304 sts.
Rnd 5 Ch 3, sc in next dc, dc in next sc, sc in next dc, (dc, sc, dc) in next sc (corner made), *sc in next dc, (dc in next sc, sc in next dc) 37 times, (dc, sc, dc) in next sc (corner made). Rep from * twice, sc in next dc, (dc in next sc, sc in next dc) to end of rnd, join rnd with sl st in top of beg-ch—312 sts.
Rnd 6 Ch 1, sc in same st as sl st, (dc in next sc, sc in next dc) twice, (dc, sc, dc) in next sc (corner made), *sc in next dc, (dc in next sc, sc in next dc) 38 times, (dc, sc, dc) in next sc; rep from * twice, (sc in next dc, dc in next sc) to end of rnd, join rnd with sl st in 1st sc—320 sts.
Rnd 7 Ch 3, sc in next dc, (dc in next sc, sc in next dc) twice, (dc, sc, dc) in next sc (corner made), *sc in next dc, (dc in next sc, sc in next dc) 39 times, (dc, sc, dc) in next sc (corner made). Rep from * twice, sc in next dc, (dc in next sc, sc in next dc) to end of rnd, join rnd with sl st in top of beg-ch—328 sts.
Rnd 8 Ch 1, sc in same st as sl st (dc in next sc, sc in next dc) 3 times, (dc, sc, dc) in next sc (corner made), *sc in next dc, (dc in next sc, sc in next dc) 40 times, (dc, sc, dc) in next sc (corner made). Rep from * twice, (sc in next dc, dc in next sc) to end of rnd, join rnd with sl st in 1st sc. Fasten off—336 sts.

Tie

Row 1 With RS facing, count 40 sts along any edge from one corner of Blanket, join B with sl st in next st, ch 1, sc in same st, sc in each of next 2 sts—3 sc. Ch 1, turn.
Row 2 Sc in each sc across. Ch 1, turn.
Rep Row 2 until tie measures 27" (68.5cm) from beg. Fasten off.
Weave in ends.

sunny squares
baby blanket

Yarn [4]

Vanna's Choice by Lion Brand Yarn Co., 3½oz/100g skeins, each approx 170yd/155m (acrylic)

- 7 skeins, 1 each in Sapphire #107 (A), Dusty Blue #108 (B), Scarlet #113 (C), Wild Berry #141 (D), Mustard #158 (E), Pea Green #170 (F), and Fern #171 (G)

Vanna's Choice Baby by Lion Brand Yarn Co., 3½oz/100g skeins, each approx 170yd/155m (acrylic)

- 3 skeins, 2 in Lamb #098 (H) and 1 in Pink Poodle #138 (I)

Hook

Size J/10 (6mm) crochet hook OR SIZE NEEDED TO OBTAIN GAUGE

Additional

- Tapestry needle

Measurements

25"/63.5cm x 30"/76cm

Gauge

Finished square is 5"/12.5cm
TAKE TIME TO CHECK YOUR GAUGE

Note

Ch-3 counts as 1 dc throughout

Blanket

Square 1 (make 4)
With I, ch 4; join with sl st in 1st ch to form a ring.

Rnd 1 (RS) Ch 3 (counts as 1 dc here and throughout), 2 dc in ring, ch 2, (3 dc in ring, ch 2) 3 times, join rnd with sl st in top of beg-ch. Fasten off. 12 dc and 4 ch-2 sps.

Rnd 2 With RS facing, join B with sl st in any ch-2 sp, ch 3, (2 dc, ch 2, 3 dc) in same ch-2 sp (corner made), ch 1, *(3 dc, ch 2, 3 dc) in next ch-2 sp (corner made), ch 1. Rep

from * 2 more times, join rnd with sl st in top of beg-ch. 4 corners and 4 ch-1 sps.

Rnd 3 Sl st in each dc across to 1st ch-2 sp, (sl st, ch 3, 2 dc, ch 2, 3 dc) in 1st ch-2 sp, ch 1, 3 dc in next ch-1 sp, ch 1, *(3 dc, ch 2, 3 dc) in next ch-2 sp, ch 1, 3 dc in next ch-1 sp, ch 1. Rep from * 2 more times, join rnd with sl st in top of beg-ch. Fasten off B. 4 corners, 8 ch-1 sps and 4 3-dc groups.

Rnd 4 With RS facing, join H with sl st in any ch-2 sp, (ch 3, 2 dc, ch 2, 3 dc) in same ch-2 sp, ch 1, (3 dc in next ch-1 sp, ch 1) twice, *(3 dc, ch 2, 3 dc) in corner ch-2 sp, ch 1, (3 dc in next ch-1 sp, ch 1) twice. Rep from * around, join rnd with sl st in top of beg-ch. Fasten off H. 4 corners, 12 ch-1 sps and 8 3-dc groups.

Make 26 more squares in the following color combinations.

Square 2 (make 4), Rnd 1 B, Rnds 2 & 3 G, Rnd 4 H; **Square 3** (make 3), Rnd 1 C, Rnds 2 & 3 I, Rnd 4 H; **Square 4** (make 3), Rnd 1 G, Rnds 2 & 3 C, Rnd 4 H;

Square 5 (make 2), Rnd 1 C, Rnds 2 & 3 D, Rnd 4 H; **Square 6**, (make 2), Rnd 1 F, Rnds 2 & 3 E, Rnd 4 H; **Square 7** (make 2), Rnd 1 D, Rnd 4 H; **Square 8** (make 2), Rnd 1 B, Rnds 2 & 3 A, Rnd 4 H;

Square 9 (make 2), Rnd 1 E, Rnds 2 & 3 G, Rnd 4 H; **Square 10** (make 1), Rnd 1 B, Rnds 2 & 3 C, Rnd 4 H; **Square 11** (make 1), Rnd 1 F, Rnds 2 & 3 I, Rnd 4 H;

Square 12 (make 1), Rnd 1 I, remaining rnds A; **Square 13** (make 1), Rnd 1 D, remaining rnds A; **Square 14** (make 1), Rnd 1 H, remaining rnds A; **Square 15** (make 1), Rnd 1 C, remaining rnds A.

Finishing

Arrange Squares as shown in diagram and sew together with a whip st using tapestry

needle and H, working in outside loops only. Weave in ends.

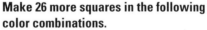

3	1	5	9	10
7	2	11	12	5
1	4	13	7	2
2	3	8	4	6
6	1	9	3	8
14	15	4	1	2

radiating granny baby blanket

Yarn

Vanna's Choice by Lion Brand Yarn Co., 3½oz/100g skeins, each approx 170yd/155m (acrylic)

- 6 skeins, 1 each in Soft Pink #103 (A), Pink #101 (B), Dusty Blue #108 (C), Colonial Blue #109 (D), Wild Berry #141 (E), and Scarlet #113 (F)

Vanna's Choice Baby by Lion Brand Yarn Co., 3½oz/100g skeins, each approx 170yd/155m (acrylic)

- 1 skein Pink Poodle #138 (G)

Hook

Size J/10 (6.0mm) crochet hook OR SIZE NEEDED TO OBTAIN GAUGE

Additional

- Tapestry needle

Measurements

28"/ 71cm square

Gauge

4 shells (if measured at base of sts) and 6 rows to 4"/10cm over pattern
TAKE TIME TO CHECK YOUR GAUGE

Note

Ch-3 counts as 1 dc throughout

Blanket
Center Square

With A, ch 4; join with sl st in 1st ch to form ring.

Rnd 1 (RS) Ch 3 (counts as 1 dc here and throughout), 2 dc in ring, ch 2, (3 dc in ring, ch 2) 3 times, join rnd with sl st in top of beg-ch. Fasten off A. 12 dc and 4 ch-2 sps.

Rnd 2 With RS facing, join B with sl st in any ch-2 sp, ch 3, (2 dc, ch 2, 3 dc) in same ch-2 sp (corner made), ch 1, *(3 dc, ch 2, 3 dc) in next ch-2 sp (corner made), ch 1. Rep from * 2 more times, join rnd with sl st in

top of beg-ch—4 ch-2 corners. Fasten off B.

Rnd 3 With RS facing, join G with sl st in any corner ch-2 sp, ch 3, (2 dc, ch 2, 3 dc) in same ch-2 sp, ch 1, 3 dc in next ch-1 sp, ch 1, *(3 dc, ch 2, 3 dc) in next ch-2 sp, ch 1, 3 dc in next ch-1 sp, ch 1. Rep from * twice more, join rnd with sl st in top of beg-ch—4 corners and one 3-dc group on each side. Fasten off G.

Rnd 4 With RS facing join C with sl st in any corner ch-2 sp, ch 3, (2 dc, ch 2, 3 dc) in same ch-2 sp, (ch 1, 3 dc in next ch-1 sp) twice, ch 1, *(3 dc, ch 2, 3 dc) in next ch-2 sp, (ch 1, 3 dc in next ch-1 sp) twice, ch 1. Rep from * twice more, join rnd with sl st in top of beg-ch—4 corners and two 3-dc groups on each side. Fasten off C.

Rnd 5 With RS facing join D with sl st in any corner ch-2 sp, ch 3, (2 dc, ch 2, 3 dc) in same ch-2 sp, ch 1, (3 dc in next ch-1 sp, ch 1) across to next corner ch-2 sp, *(3 dc, ch 2, 3 dc) in next ch-2 sp, ch 1, (3 dc in next ch-1 sp, ch 1) across to next corner ch-2 sp. Rep from * twice more, join rnd with sl st in

top of beg-ch. Fasten off D.

Rnds 6–12 Rep Rnd 5 in the following color order, ending off each color at the end of the rnd. E, F, A, B, G, C, D. 4 corners and 10 3-dc groups on each side at end of Rnd 12.

Panel 1

Row 1 (RS) With RS facing, join E with sl st in any corner ch-2 sp, ch 3, dc in same ch-2 sp, ch 1, (3 dc in next ch-1 sp, ch 1) across to next corner ch-2 sp, 2 dc in next corner ch-2 sp—11 3-dc groups and 1 2-dc group at each end. Change to F, ch 3, turn.

Row 2 (WS) With F, ch 3 (counts as dc), turn, 3 dc in next ch-1 sp, (ch 1, 3 dc in next ch-1 sp) across to end of row, dc in top of beg-ch. Change to A, ch 3, turn. 12 3-dc groups and one dc at each end.

Row 3 Dc in 1st dc, ch 1, (3 dc in next ch-1 sp, ch 1) across to end of row, 2 dc in top of beg ch. Change to B, ch 3, turn.

Row 4 With B, rep Row 2. Change to G at the end of row.

Row 5 With G, rep Row 3. Change to C at

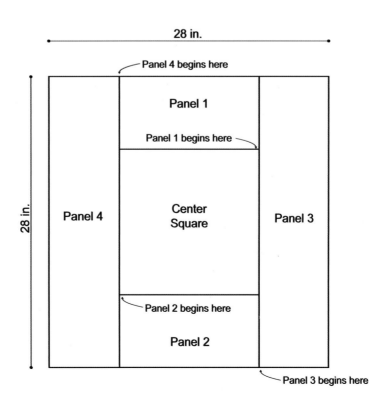

28 in.

Panel 4 begins here

Panel 1

Panel 1 begins here

28 in.

Panel 4

Center Square

Panel 3

Panel 2 begins here

Panel 2

Panel 3 begins here

the end of row.
Row 6 With C, rep Row 2. Change to D at the end of row.
Row 7 With D, rep Row 3. Change to E at the end of row.
Row 8 With E, rep Row 2. Change to F at the end of row.
Row 9 With F, rep Row 3. Change to A at the end of row.
Row 10 With A, rep Row 2. Fasten off A.

Panel 2
With RS facing, join E with sl st in corner ch–2 sp of edge opposite from Panel 1.
Rep instructions for Panel 1.

Panel 3
Row 1 With RS facing and working in ends of rows across edge of Panel 2, join E with sl st in end of last row of Panel 2, ch 3, dc in end of same row, ch 1, sk end of next row, (3 dc in end of next row, ch 1, sk end of next row) 4 times, 3 dc in corner ch–2 sp of Center

Square, ch 1, (3 dc in next ch–1 sp, ch 1) across to next corner ch–2 sp of Center Square, 3 dc in next corner ch–2 sp; working across edge of Panel 1, (ch 1, sk end of next row, 3 dc in end of next row) 4 times, ch 1, sk end of next row, 2 dc in end of last row. Change to F, ch 3, turn. 21 3–dc groups and one 2–dc group at each end.
Row 2 (3 dc in next ch–1 sp, ch 1) across to end, dc in top of beg–ch. Change to A, ch 3, turn. 22 3–dc groups and one dc at each end.
Row 3 Dc in 1st dc, ch 1, (3 dc in next ch–1 sp, ch 1) across to end, 2 dc in top of beg–ch. Change to B, ch 3, turn.
Row 4: With B, rep Row 2. Change to G at the end of row.
Row 5: With G, rep Row 3. Change to C at the end of row.
Row 6: With C, rep Row 2. Change to D at the end of row.
Row 7: With D, rep Row 3. Change to E at the end of row.
Row 8: With E, rep Row 2. Change to F at the end of row.
Row 9: With F, rep Row 3. Change to A at the end of row.
Row 10: With A, rep Row 2. Fasten off A.

Panel 4
Row 1 With RS facing and working in ends of rows across edge of Panel 1, join E with sl st in end of last row of Panel 1, ch 3, dc in end of same row, ch 1, sk end of next row, (3 dc in end of next row, ch 1, sk end of next row) 4 times, 3 dc in corner ch–2 sp of Center Square, ch 1, (3 dc in next ch–1 sp, ch 1) across to next corner ch–2 sp of Center Square, 3 dc in next corner ch–2 sp; working in ends of rows across edge of Panel 2, (ch 1, sk end of next row, 3 dc in end of next row) 4 times, ch 1, sk end of next row, 2 dc in end of last row. Change to F, ch 3, turn—21 3–dc groups and one 2–dc group at each end.
Rows 2–10 Rep Rows 2–10 of Panel 3. Fasten off.

Finishing
Edging
With RS facing, join B with sc in any st along outside edge of Blanket. Work sc evenly spaced around entire blanket, working 3 sc in each corner, join rnd with sl st in 1st sc.
Fasten off.
Weave in ends.

flowery blankie

Yarn

Vanna's Choice Baby by Lion Brand Yarn Co., 3½oz/100g skeins, each approx 170yd/155m (acrylic)

- 3 skeins, 1 each in Duckie #157 (A), Lamb #098 (B), and Sweet Pea #169 (C)

Vanna's Choice by Lion Brand Yarn Co., 3½oz/100g skeins, each approx 170yd/155m (acrylic)

- 3 skeins, 1 each in Mustard #158 (D), Fern #171 (E), and Pea Green #170 (F)

Hook
Size K/10½ (6.5mm) crochet hook OR SIZE NEEDED TO OBTAIN GAUGE

Additional
- Tapestry needle

Measurements
30"/76cm x 30"/76cm

Gauge
Finished flower is 3"/7.5cm
TAKE TIME TO CHECK YOUR GAUGE

Stitch Glossary

Cl (cluster) Yo twice, insert hook in indicated st and draw up loop, (yo, draw through 2 loops on hook) twice, (2 loops rem on hook), *yo twice, insert hook in same st and draw up loop, (yo, draw through 2 loops on hook) twice. Rep from * once more, yo, draw through all 4 loops on hook.

Blanket

Flower (make 144—24 each with A, B, C, D, E, and F)
Ch 4, sl st in 1st ch to form ring.
Rnd 1 Ch 1, 12 sc in ring; join rnd

with sl st in 1st sc.
Rnd 2 *(Sl st, ch 3, Cl, ch 3, sl st) in next sc, sl st in next sc. Rep from * 5 more times. 6 petals.
Fasten off, leaving a long yarn tail for sewing.

Finishing
Arrange flowers as shown in diagram and sew together with a whip st using tapestry needle and coordinating color. Assemble into 12 strips of 12 flowers each, then attach strips into blanket. Weave in ends.

Arrange and sew together a total of 12 Strips of 12 Flowers each

circle in a square baby blanket

Yarn

Vanna's Choice by Lion Brand Yarn Co., 3½oz/100g skeins, each approx 170yd/155m (acrylic)

- 5 skeins, 1 each in Sapphire #107 (A), Scarlet #113 (B), Kelly Green #172 (C), Colonial Blue #109 (D), and Fern #171 (E)

Vanna's Choice Baby by Lion Brand Yarn Co., 3½oz/100g skeins, each approx 170yd/155m (acrylic)

- 1 skein in Lamb #098 (F)

Hook

Size J/10 (6mm) crochet hook OR SIZE NEEDED TO OBTAIN GAUGE

Additional

- Tapestry needle

Measurements

24"/61cm x 29"/73.5cm

Gauge

Finished square is 5½"/14 cm
TAKE TIME TO CHECK YOUR GAUGE

Notes

1 Ch-3 counts as 1 dc throughout.
2 To change color, work last st of old color to last yarn over. Yarn over with new color and draw through all loops on hook to complete st. Fasten off old color.

Blanket

Square 1 (make 5)

With A ch 4, join rnd with sl st in 1st ch to form ring.
Rnd 1 Ch 3 (counts as 1 dc here and throughout), 11 dc in ring, join with sl st in top of beg-ch—12 dc.
Rnd 2 Ch 3, dc in same dc as sl st, 2 dc in each dc around, join rnd with sl st in top of beg-ch—24 dc.
Rnd 3 With B, ch 1, sc in same st as sl st, sc in next dc, hdc in each of next dc, 3 dc in next dc, hdc in next dc, sc in next dc, *sc in each of next 2 dc, hdc in next dc, 3 dc in next dc, hdc in next dc, sc in next dc. Rep from * twice more; join rnd with sl st in 1st sc—32 sts.
Rnd 4 Ch 3, dc in each of next 3 sts, 5 dc in next st, dc in each of next 3 sts, *dc in each of next 4 sts, 5 dc in next st, dc in each of next 3 sts. Rep from * twice more, join rnd with sl st in top of beg-ch—48 sts.
Rnd 5 With F, ch 3, dc in each of next 5 dc, 5 dc in next dc, dc in each of next 5 dc, *dc in each of next 6 dc, 5 dc in next dc, dc in each of next 5 dc. Rep from * 2 more times; join with sl st in top of beg-ch. 64 dc.
Fasten off.

Square 2 (make 5)

Rep Square 1, using C for Rnds 1 & 2, D for Rnds 3 & 4, and A for Rnd 5.

Square 3 (make 5)

Rep Square 1, using E for Rnds 1 & 2, C for Rnds 3 & 4, and D for Rnd 5.

Square 4 (make 5)

Rep Square 1, using F for Rnds 1 & 2, E for Rnds 3 & 4, and C for Rnd 5.

Finishing

Arrange Squares as shown in diagram and sew together with a whip st using tapestry needle and yarn that matches squares being sewn, working in outside loops only.

Border

With RS facing, join B with a sl st anywhere along outside edge of Blanket.
Rnd 1 Ch 3, work dcs evenly spaced around entire outside edge of Blanket, working 3 dc in each corner, join rnd with sl st in top of beg-ch. Fasten off.
Rnd 2 Join F with a sl st in any st of Rnd 1 of Border. Ch 1, sc in each dc around, working 3 sc in center dc at each corner, join rnd with sl st in 1st sc. Fasten off.
Weave in ends.

1	2	3	4
2	3	4	1
3	4	1	2
4	1	2	3
1	2	3	4

patchwork squares baby blanket

Yarn

Vanna's Choice by Lion Brand Yarn Co., 3½oz/100g skeins, each approx 170yd/155m (acrylic)
- 5 skeins, 1 each in Pink #101 (A), Soft Pink #103 (B), Beige #123 (C), Terracotta #134 (D), and Rose #142 (E)

Vanna's Choice Baby by Lion Brand Yarn Co., 3½oz/100g skeins, each approx 170yd/155m (acrylic)
- 2 skeins, 1 each in Goldfish #132 (F) and Pink Poodle #138 (G)

Hook
Size J/10 (6mm) crochet hook OR SIZE NEEDED TO OBTAIN GAUGE

Additional
- Tapestry needle

Measurements
25"/63.5cm x 31"/78.5cm

Gauges
Finished small square is 3"/7.5cm; finished large square is 6"/15cm
TAKE TIME TO CHECK YOUR GAUGE

Note
Ch-3 counts as 1 dc throughout

Stitch Glossary
beg-Cl (beg cluster) Ch 2, yo, insert hook in indicated sp and draw up loop, yo, draw through 2 loops on hook (2 loops rem on hook); yo, insert hook in same sp and draw up loop, yo, draw through 2 loops on hook, yo, draw through all 3 loops on hook.
Cl (cluster) Yo, insert hook in indicated sp and draw up loop, yo, draw through 2 loops on hook (2 loops rem on hook), *yo, insert hook in same sp and draw up loop, yo, draw through 2 loops on hook. Rep from * once more, yo, draw through all loops on hook.

Blanket
Small Square (make 20—2 each with A and D, 3 each with B, C, E, and G, and 4 with F)
Make an adjustable ring as follows:

Adjustable Ring Method
Wrap yarn around index finger. Insert hook into ring on finger, yarn over and draw up a loop. Carefully slip ring from finger and work the stitches of Rnd 1 into the ring. When Rnd 1 is complete, gently but firmly pull tail to tighten center of ring.
Rnd 1 (RS) (Beg-Cl, ch 3, Cl) in ring, ch 1, *(Cl, ch 3, Cl) in ring, ch 1. Rep from * twice more, join rnd with sl st in top of Beg-Cl—8 Cl, 4 ch-3 sps and 4 ch-1 sps.
Rnd 2 (Sl st, Beg-Cl, ch 3, Cl) in first ch-3 sp (corner made), ch 2, 2 dc in next ch-1 sp, ch 2, *(Cl, ch 3, Cl) in next ch-3 sp (corner made), ch 2, 2 dc in next ch-1 sp, ch 2; rep from * 2 more times; join with sl st in top of Beg-Cl—8 Cl, 8 dc and 4 corner ch-3 sps. Fasten off.

Large Square (make 15—2 each with A, B, C, D, E and F, and 3 with G)
Make an adjustable ring.
Rnd 1 (RS) (Beg-Cl, ch 5, Cl) in ring, ch 2, *(Cl, ch 5, Cl) in ring, ch 2. Rep from * twice more, join rnd with sl st in top of Beg-Cl—8 Cl, 4 ch-5 sps and 4 ch-2 sps.
Rnd 2 (Sl st, Beg-Cl, ch 3, Cl) in first ch-5 sp (corner made), ch 2, 3 dc in next ch-2 sp, ch 2, *(Cl, ch 3, Cl) in next ch-5 sp (corner made), ch 2, 3 dc in next ch-2 sp, ch 2. Rep from * twice more, join rnd with sl st in top of Beg-Cl—8 Cl, 12 dc and 4 corner ch-3 sps.
Rnds 3 & 4 (Sl st, Beg-Cl, ch 3, Cl) in first ch-3 sp, ch 2, 2 dc in next ch-2 sp, dc in each dc across to next ch-2 sp, 2 dc in next ch-2 sp, ch 2, *(Cl, ch 3, Cl) in next ch-3 sp, ch 2, 2 dc in next ch-2 sp, dc in each dc across to next ch-2 sp, 2 dc in next ch-2 sp, ch 2. Rep from * twice more, join rnd with sl st in top of Beg-Cl—8 Cl, 28 dc and 4 corner ch-3 sps after Rnd 3; 8 Cl, 44 dc and 4 corner ch-3 sps after Rnd 4. Fasten off after Rnd 4.

Finishing
Arrange Squares as shown in diagram and sew together with a whip st using tapestry needle and yarn that matches squares being sewn, working in outside loops only.

Edging
Rnd 1 With RS facing, join A with sl st in any st along outside edge of Blanket, ch 1, sc evenly spaced around, working 3 sc in each corner, join rnd with sl st in first sc.
Rnd 2 Ch 1, sc in each sc around, working 3 sc in center sc at each corner, join rnd with sl st in first sc. Fasten off.
Weave in ends.

double shell baby blanket

Yarn

Vanna's Choice by Lion Brand Yarn Co., 3½oz/100g skeins, each approx 170yd/155m (acrylic)

- 7 skeins, 1 each in Pea Green #170 (A), Kelly Green #172 (B), Dusty Blue #108 (C), Sapphire #107 (D), Colonial Blue #109 (E), Eggplant #145 (F), and Wild Berry #141 (G)

Vanna's Choice Baby by Lion Brand Yarn Co., 3½oz/100g skeins, each approx 170yd/155m (acrylic)

- 3 skeins, 1 each in Duckie #157 (H), Berrylicious #139 (I), and Pink Poodle #138 (J)

Hook

Size P/15 (10mm) crochet hook OR SIZE NEEDED TO OBTAIN GAUGE

Additional

- Tapestry needle

Measurements

28"/71cm x 34"/86.5cm

Gauge

1 patt rep to 3½"/9cm and 4 rows to 4½"/11.5cm over pattern with 2 strands of yarn held together
TAKE TIME TO CHECK YOUR GAUGE

Notes

1 Ch-3 counts as 1 dc throughout.
2 Blanket is worked with 2 strands of yarn held together throughout.

Stitch Glossary

dc4tog (dc 4 sts tog) (Yo, insert hook in next st and draw up loop, yo, draw through 2 loops) 4 times, yo, draw through all 5 loops on hook.

dc5tog (dc 5 sts tog) (Yo, insert hook in next st and draw up loop, yo, draw through 2 loops) 5 times, yo, draw through all 6 loops on hook.

dc9tog (dc 9 sts tog) (Yo, insert hook in next st and draw up loop, yo, draw through 2 loops) 9 times, yo, draw through all 10 loops on hook.

Blanket

With 1 strand each of A and H held tog, ch 66.
Row 1 Sc in 2nd ch from hook, *sk 3 ch, 9 dc in next ch, sk 3 ch, sc in next ch. Rep from * across. Fasten off H, pick up B, ch 3, turn. 8 patt reps.
Row 2 Sk 1st st, dc4tog (counts as a dc5tog including beg ch-3), ch 3, sc in next dc (center dc of 9-dc group), *ch 3, dc9tog, ch 3, sc in next dc. Rep from * across to last 5 sts, ch 3, dc5tog. Fasten off A, pick up C, ch 3, turn.
Row 3 4 dc in 1st st, sk next ch-3 sp, sc in next sc, *sk next ch-3 sp, 9 dc in next st, sk next ch-3 sp, sc in next sc. Rep from * across to last ch-3 sp, sk last ch-3 sp, 5 dc in last st. Fasten off B, pick up D, ch 1, turn.
Row 4 Sc in first st, *ch 3, dc9tog, ch 3, sc in next dc (center dc of 9-dc group); rep from * across, working final sc into top of turning ch-3. Fasten off C, pick up E, ch 1, turn.
Row 5 Sc in first sc, *sk next ch-3 sp, 9 dc in next st, sk next ch-3 sp, sc in next sc; rep from * across. Continue to change color as before, dropping and fastening off one strand of the old color combination and picking up one new strand to form the next color combination before the turning ch.
Row 6 With 1 strand each of E and F held tog, rep Row 2.
Row 7 With 1 strand each of F and G held tog, rep Row 3.
Row 8 With 1 strand each of G and I held tog, rep Row 4.
Row 9 With 1 strand each of I and J held tog, rep Row 5.
Row 10 With 1 strand each of J and H held tog, rep Row 2.
Row 11 With 1 strand each of H and A held tog, rep Row 3.
Row 12 With 1 strand each of A and B held tog, rep Row 4.
Row 13 With 1 strand each of B and C held tog, rep Row 5.
Row 14 With 1 strand each of C and D held tog, rep Row 2.
Row 15 With 1 strand each of D and E held tog, rep Row 3.
Row 16 With 1 strand each of E and F held tog, rep Row 4.
Row 17 With 1 strand each of F and G held tog, rep Row 5.
Row 18 With 1 strand each of G and I held tog, rep Row 2.
Row 19 With 1 strand each of I and J held tog, rep Row 3.
Row 20 With 1 strand each of J and H held tog, rep Row 4.
Row 21 With 1 strand each of H and A held tog, rep Row 5.
Rows 22–30 Repeat Rows 2–10. Fasten off.

Finishing

Weave in ends.

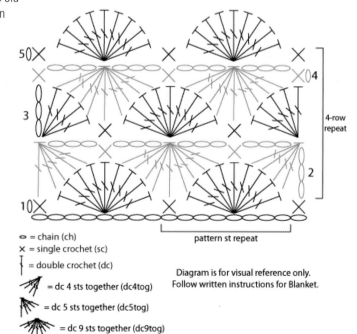

○ = chain (ch)
✕ = single crochet (sc)
⌡ = double crochet (dc)
⌇ = dc 4 sts together (dc4tog)
⌇ = dc 5 sts together (dc5tog)
⌇ = dc 9 sts together (dc9tog)

Diagram is for visual reference only. Follow written instructions for Blanket.

pattern st repeat

4-row repeat

graphic triangles
baby blanket

Yarn

Vanna's Choice by Lion Brand
Yarn Co., 3½oz/100g skeins,
each approx 170yd/155m
(acrylic)

- 4 skeins, 2 each in Dusty Blue #108 (A), and Linen #099 (B)

Hook

Size J/10 (6mm) crochet hook OR
SIZE NEEDED TO OBTAIN GAUGE

Additional

- 6 yarn bobbins
- Tapestry needle

Measurements

23½"/60cm x 29½/74cm

Gauge

11 sts and 9 rows to 4½/10cm over hdc
TAKE TIME TO CHECK YOUR GAUGE

Notes

1 Ch-2 counts as 1 hdc throughout.
2 To change color, work last st of old color to last yo. Yarn over with new color and draw through all loops to complete st. Do not fasten off old color.
3 Wind 6 bobbins for two-color rows, 3 each in A and B.

Blanket

With A, ch 65.
Row 1 (RS) Hdc in 3rd ch from hook and in each ch across—64 hdc. Ch 2, turn—ch-2 counts as 1 hdc here and throughout.
Row 2 Hdc in each of next 14 hdc, with B, hdc in next hdc *with A, hdc in each of next 15 hdc, with B, hdc in next hdc. Rep from * twice more. Ch 2, turn.

Row 3 Hdc in each of next 2 hdc, with A, hdc in each of next 13 hdc, *with B, hdc in each of next 3 hdc, with A, hdc in each of next 13 hdc. Rep from * twice more, ch 2, turn.
Row 4 Hdc in each of next 12 hdc, with B, hdc in each of next 3 hdc, *with A, hdc in next each of next 13 hdc; with B, hdc in next 3 hdc; rep from * twice more, ch 2, turn.
Row 5 Hdc in each of next 4 hdc, with A, hdc in each of next 11 hdc; *with B, hdc in each of next 5 hdc, with A, hdc in each of next 11 hdc. Rep from * twice more, ch 2, turn.
Row 6 Hdc in each of next 10 hdc; with B, hdc in each of next 5 hdc; *with A, hdc in each of next 11 hdc, with B, hdc in each of next 5 hdc. Rep from * twice more, ch 2, turn.
Row 7 Hdc in each of next 6 hdc, with A, hdc in each of next 9 hdc, *with B, hdc in each of next 7 hdc, with A, hdc in each of next 9 hdc. Rep from * twice more, ch 2, turn.
Row 8 Hdc in each of next 8 hdc, with B, hdc in each of next 7 hdc; *with A, hdc in each of next 9 hdc, with B, hdc in each of next 7 hdc. Rep from * twice more, ch 2, turn.
Row 9 Hdc in each of next 8 hdc, with A, hdc in each of next 7 hdc, *with B, hdc in each of next 9 hdc, with A, hdc in each of next 7 hdc. Rep from * twice more, ch 2, turn.
Row 10 Hdc in each of next 6 hdc, with B, hdc in each of next 9 hdc, *with A, hdc in next each of next 7 hdc, with B, hdc in each of next 9 hdc. Rep from * twice more, ch 2, turn.
Row 11 Hdc in each of next 10 hdc, with A, hdc in each of next 5 hdc, *with B, hdc in each of next 11 hdc, with A, hdc in each of next 5 hdc. Rep from * twice more, ch 2, turn.
Row 12 Hdc in each of next 4 hd, with B, hdc in each of next 11 hdc, *with A, hdc in

each of next 5 hdc, with B, hdc in each of next 11 hdc. Rep from * twice more, ch 2, turn.
Row 13 Hdc in each of next 12 hdc, with A, hdc in each of next 3 hdc, *with B, hdc in each of next 13 hdc, with A, hdc in each of next 3 hdc. Rep from * twice more, ch 2, turn.
Row 14 Hdc in each of next 2 hdc, with B, hdc in each of next 13 hdc, *with A, hdc in each of next 3 hdc; with B, hdc in each of next 13 hdc. Rep from * twice more, ch 2, turn.
Row 15 Hdc in each of next 14 hdc, with A, hdc in next hdc; *with B, hdc in each of next 15 hdc, with A, hdc in next hdc. Rep from * twice more, change to B, ch 2, turn.
Row 16 With B, hdc in each hdc across. Change to A, ch 2, turn.
Row 17 With A, hdc in each hdc across. Ch 2, turn.
Rows 18–64 Rep Rows 2–17 twice, then Rows 2–16 once more.
Fasten off after Row 64.

Finishing
Edging

Note: Edging is worked around entire outside edge of blanket, using B when working into B-colored sts, and A when working into A-colored sts. One long edge and one short edge are B colored, and one long edge and one short edge are A colored.
With RS facing, join B with sl st at beg of the two B-colored edges, ch 1, (sc evenly across edge to corner, 3 sc in corner) twice, change to A, (sc evenly across edge to corner, 3 sc in corner) twice, join rnd with sl st in 1st sc.
Fasten off.
Weave in ends.

crochet circle baby blanket

Yarn

Vanna's Choice by Lion Brand Yarn Co., 3½oz/100g skeins, each approx 170yd/155m (acrylic)
- 4 skeins, 1 each in Soft Pink #103 (A), Pink #101 (B), Pea Green #170 (C), and Chocolate #126 (D)

Vanna's Choice Baby by Lion Brand Yarn Co., 3½oz/100g skeins, each approx 170yd/155m (acrylic)
- 1 skein in Pink Poodle #138 (E)

Hook
Size P/15 (10mm) crochet hook OR SIZE NEEDED TO OBTAIN GAUGE

Additional
- Tapestry needle

Measurements
28"/71cm in diameter

Gauge
5 rows and 10 sts to 6"/15cm in dc
TAKE TIME TO CHECK YOUR GAUGE

Notes
1 Ch-3 counts as 1 dc throughout.
2 Blanket is worked with 2 strands of yarn held tog throughout.
3 To change color, fasten off one strand of the previous color combination and pick up one strand of the new color to create the next color combination.

Blanket
With 1 strand each of A and B held tog, make an adjustable ring as follows:

Wrap yarn around index finger. Insert hook into ring on finger, yarn over and draw up a loop. Carefully slip ring from finger and work the stitches of Rnd 1 into the ring. When Rnd 1 is complete, gently but firmly, pull tail to tighten center of ring.

Rnd 1 (RS) Ch 3 (counts as 1 dc here and throughout), work 11 dc in ring; join with sl st in top of beg-ch— 12 dc. Fasten off A. Leaving a long beg tail to weave in later, pick up D.
Rnd 2 With 1 strand each of B and D held tog, ch 3, dc in same st as join, 2 dc in each dc around; join with sl st in top of beg-ch— 24 dc. Fasten off B, pick up E.
Rnd 3 With 1 strand each of D and E held tog, ch 3, dc in same st as join, dc in next dc, *2 dc in next dc, dc in next dc. Rep from * around, join rnd with sl st in top of beg-ch—36 dc. Fasten off D, pick up C. Continue changing colors as before, ending off one color and picking up one new color at the end of every rnd.
Rnd 4 With E and C, ch 3, dc in same st as join, dc in each of next 2 dc, *2 dc in next dc, dc in each of next 2 dc. Rep from * around, join rnd with sl st in top of beg-ch—48 dc.
Rnd 5 With C and A, ch 3, dc in same st as join, dc in each of next 3 dc, *2 dc in next dc, dc in each of next 3 dc. Rep from * around, join rnd with sl st in top of beg-ch—60 dc.
Rnd 6 With A and B ch 3, dc in same st as join, dc in each of next 4 dc, *2 dc in next dc dc in each of next 4 dc. Rep from * around, join rnd with sl st in top of beg-ch—72 dc.
Rnd 7 With B and D ch 3, dc in same st as join, dc in each of next 5 dc, *2 dc in next dc, dc in each of next 5 dc. Rep from * around, join rnd with sl st in top of beg-ch—84 sts.
Rnd 8 With D and E ch 3, dc in same st as join, dc in each of next 6 dc, *2 dc in next dc, dc in each of next 6 dc. Rep from * around, join rnd with sl st in top of beg-ch—96 sts.
Rnd 9 With E and C ch 3, dc in same st as join, dc in each of next 7 dc, *2 dc in next dc, dc in each of next 7 dc. Rep from * around, join rnd with sl st in top of beg-ch—108 sts.
Rnd 10 With C and A ch 3, dc in same st as join, dc in each of next 8 dc, *2 dc in next dc, dc in each of next 8 dc. Rep from * around, join rnd with sl st in top of beg-ch—120 sts.
Rnd 11 With A and B ch 3, dc in same st as join, dc in each of next 9 dc, *2 dc in next dc, dc in each of next 9 dc. Rep from * around, join rnd with sl st in top of beg-ch—132 sts.
Rnd 12 With B and D ch 3, dc in same st as join, dc in each of next 10 dc *2 dc in next dc, dc in each of next 10 dc. Rep from * around, join rnd with sl st in top of beg-ch—144 sts.
Fasten off.

Finishing
Weave in ends.

electric squares
baby blanket

Yarn

Vanna's Choice by Lion Brand
Yarn Co., 3½oz/100g skeins,
each approx 170yd/155m
(acrylic)

- 5 skeins, 1 each in Sapphire
  #107(A), Chocolate #126 (B),
  Terracotta #134 (C), Wild
  Berry #141 (D), and Mustard
  #158 (E)

Vanna's Choice Baby by Lion
Brand Yarn Co., 3½oz/100g
skeins, each approx
170yd/155m (acrylic)

- 4 skeins, 1 each in Goldfish
  #132 (F), Pink Poodle #138
  (G), Berrylicious #139 (H), and
  Sweet Pea #169 (I)

Hook
Size J/10 (6mm) crochet hook
OR SIZE NEEDED TO OBTAIN
GAUGE

Additional
- Tapestry needle

Measurements
26"/66cm x 26"/66cm

Gauge
Finished square = 3¾"/9.5cm square
TAKE TIME TO CHECK YOUR GAUGE

Note
Ch-3 counts as 1 dc throughout

2	3	11	17	7	1	16
8	1	6	2	10	3	4
3	2	13	4	5	1	9
12	5	1	3	8	2	6
7	8	2	10	4	15	1
4	14	3	1	9	7	2
1	6	9	5	2	11	10

Jack Deutsch

Blanket
Square 1 (make 7)
With H, ch 4; join with sl st
in 1st ch to form ring.
Rnd 1 (RS) Ch 3 (counts as
1st dc here and throughout), 2 dc in ring, ch
2, (3 dc in ring, ch 2) 3 times; join rnd with
sl st in top of beg-ch— 12 dc and 4 ch-2
sps. Fasten off H.
Rnd 2 With RS facing, join E with sl st in
any ch-2 sp, ch 3, (2 dc, ch 2, 3 dc) in same
ch-2 sp (corner made), ch 1, *(3 dc, ch 2, 3
dc) in next ch-2 sp (corner made), ch 1; rep
from * 2 more times; join rnd with sl st in
top of beg-ch—4 corners and 4 ch-1 sps.
Rnd 3 Sl st in each dc across to 1st ch-2
sp, (sl st, ch 3, 2 dc, ch 2, 3 dc) in 1st ch-2
sp, ch 1, 3 dc in next ch-1 sp, ch 1, *(3 dc,
ch 2, 3 dc) in next ch-2 sp, ch 1, 3 dc in next
ch-1 sp, ch 1; rep from * 2 more times; join
rnd with sl st in top of beg-ch—4 corners, 8
ch-1 sps and four 3-dc groups. Fasten off E.

Make 42 more squares in the following color combinations.
Square 2 (make 7), Rnd 1 D, remain-
ing rnds F; **Square 3** (make 5), Rnd 1 G,
remaining rnds D; **Square 4** (make 4),
Rnd 1 B, remaining rnds G; **Square 5** (make
3), Rnd 1 C, remaining rnds H;
Square 6, (make 3), Rnd 1 E, remaining rnds B; **Square 7** (make 3), Rnd 1 C,
remaining rnds B; **Square 8** (make 3), Rnd 1
F, remaining rnds I; **Square 9** (make 3), Rnd
1 A, remaining rnds I; **Square 10** (make 3),
Rnd 1 E, remaining rnds C;
Square 11 (make 2), Rnd 1 I, remaining rnds G; **Square 12** (make 1), Rnd 1 I,
remaining rnds A; **Square 13** (make 1), Rnd
1 D, remaining rnds A; **Square 14** (make 1),
Rnd 1 H, remaining rnds A;
Square 15 (make 1), Rnd 1 C, remaining rnds A; **Square 16** (make 1), Rnd 1 B,
remaining rnds A; **Square 17** (make 1), Rnd
1 A, remaining rnds, H.

Finishing
Arrange Squares as shown in diagram and
sew together with a whip st using tapestry
needle and B, working in outside loops only.
Weave in ends.

ripple baby blanket

Yarn

Vanna's Choice Baby by Lion Brand Yarn Co., 3½oz/100g skeins, each approx 170yd/155m (acrylic)

- 2 skeins, 1 each in Lamb #098 (A) and Sweet Pea #169 (B)

Vanna's Choice by Lion Brand Yarn Co., 3½oz/100g skeins, each approx 170yd/155m (acrylic)

- 5 skeins, 1 each in Fern #171 (C), Kelly Green #172 (D), Dusty Blue #108 (E), Colonial Blue #109 (F), and Sapphire #107 (G)

Hook

Size J/10 (6mm) crochet hook OR SIZE NEEDED TO OBTAIN GAUGE

Additional

- Tapestry needle

Jack Deutsch

Measurements

30"/76cm x 34"/86.5cm

Gauge

1 ripple to 5"/13cm, 5 rows to 4"/10cm over ripple pattern in dc
TAKE TIME TO CHECK YOUR GAUGE

Notes

1 Ch-3 counts as 1 dc throughout.
2 To change color, work last st of old color to last yo. Yo with new color and draw through all loops on hook to complete st. Fasten off old color.

Stitch Glossary

dc2tog (dc 2 sts together) (Yo, insert hook in next st and draw up loop, yo, draw through 2 loops on hook) twice, yo, draw through all 3 loops on hook.

Color sequence

Work 3 rows each in sequence, *A, B, C, D, E, F, G. Rep from * once more.

Afghan

With A, ch 114.
Row 1 Dc in 4th ch from hook, dc2tog 3 times, 2 dc in each of next 6 ch, *dc2tog 6 times, 2 dc in each of next 6 ch. Rep from * across to last 8 ch, dc2tog 3 times, dc in each of last 2 ch. Ch 3, turn—6 ripples.
Rows 2 & 3 Sk first dc, dc in next dc, dc2tog 3 times, 2 dc in each of next 6 dc, *dc2tog 6 times, 2 dc in each of next 6 dc. Rep from * across to last 8 dc, dc2tog 3 times, dc in next dc, dc in top of t-ch. Ch 3, turn after Row 2; change to B, ch 3, turn after Row 3.
Rep Row 2 for pattern until 42 rows have

been completed, remembering to change colors in sequence above. Fasten off after Row 42.

Finishing
Border

Join B with sl st anywhere on edge of Blanket.
Rnd 1 Ch 1, sc evenly spaced around entire outer edge, working 3 sc in each corner; join with sl st in first sc. Fasten off. Weave in ends.

colorful hexagon
baby blanket

Yarn

Vanna's Choice by Lion Brand
Yarn Co., 3½oz/100g skeins,
each approx 170yd/155m
(acrylic)
- 5 skeins, 1 each in Terracotta
  #134 (A), Soft Pink #103 (B),
  Mustard #158 (C), Fern #171
  (E), and Sapphire #107 (F)

Vanna's Choice Baby by Lion
Brand Yarn Co., 3½oz/100g
skeins, each approx 170yd/155m
(acrylic)
- 1 skein Pink Poodle #138 (D)

Hook
Size J/10 (6mm) crochet hook OR
SIZE NEEDED TO OBTAIN GAUGE

Additional
- Tapestry needle

Measurements
24"/61cm x 27"/68.5 cm

Gauge
Finished hexagon is 5¾"/14.5cm
TAKE TIME TO CHECK YOUR GAUGE

Stitch Glossary
3-dc Cl (3 double crochet cluster) Yo,
insert hook in indicated st, yo, draw up
loop, yo, draw through 2 loops on hook (2
loops rem on hook), (yo, insert hook in same
st, yo, draw up loop, yo, draw through 2
loops on hook) twice, (4 loops rem on hook)
yo, draw through all loops on hook.
4-dc Cl (4 double crochet cluster) Yo,
insert hook in indicated st, yo, draw up
loop, yo, draw through 2 loops on hook
(2 loops rem on hook), (yo, insert hook in
same st, yo, draw up loop, yo, draw through
2 loops on hook) 3 times (5 loops rem on
hook) yo, draw through all loops on hook.

Blanket
Hexagon I (make 4)
With A, ch 6, join rnd with sl st in 1st ch to
form ring.
Rnd 1 (RS) Ch 2, 3-dc Cl in ring, (ch 3, 4-dc
Cl in ring) 5 times, ch 3, join rnd with sl st
in top of 1st Cl. Fasten off A. 6 Cl.
Rnd 2 With RS facing, join B with sl st in
any ch-3 sp, ch 2, (3-dc Cl, ch 3, 4-dc Cl) in
same ch–3 sp (corner made), *ch 3, (4-dc
Cl, ch 3, 4-dc Cl) in next ch-3 sp (corner
made). Rep from * 4 more times, ch 3,
join rnd with sl st in top of 1st Cl—12 Cl.
Fasten off B.
Rnd 3 With RS facing, join C with sl st in
any corner ch-3 sp, ch 2, (3-dc Cl, ch 3, 4-dc
Cl) in same ch-3 sp (corner made), ch 3,
4-dc Cl in next ch-3 sp, *ch 3, (4-dc Cl, ch 3,
4-dc Cl) in next ch-3 sp (corner made), ch 3,
4-dc Cl in next ch-3 sp.
Rep from * 4 more times, ch 3, join rnd with
sl st in top of 1st Cl—18 Cl.
Fasten off.

Hexagon II (make 4)
Make same as Hexagon I, using B for Rnd
1, C for Rnd 2, D for Rnd 3.

Hexagon III (make 4)
Make same as Hexagon I, using C for Rnd
1, D for Rnd 2, E for Rnd 3.

Hexagon IV (make 4)
Make same as Hexagon I, using D for
Rnd 1, E for Rnd 2, F for Rnd 3.

Hexagon V (make 4)
Make same as Hexagon I, using E for
Rnd 1, F for Rnd 2, A for Rnd 3.

Hexagon VI (make 3)
Make same as Hexagon I, using F for
Rnd 1, A for Rnd 2, B for Rnd 3.

Finishing
Arrange motifs as shown in diagram
and sew together with a whip st using
tapestry needle and yarn that matches
squares being sewn, working in outside
loops only. Weave in ends.

Border
From RS, join C with sl st anywhere along
outside edge of Blanket.
Note To space the sc evenly and keep the
border flat, work 2 or 3 sc in each outer
point and skip 1 or 2 sc at each inside
corner.
Rnd 1 Ch 1, work sc evenly spaced around
entire outside edge of Blanket; join with sl
st in 1st sc. Fasten off.
Weave in ends.

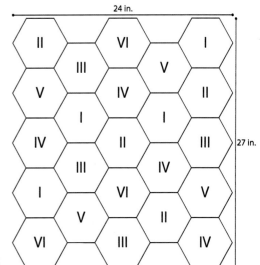

swaddling blanket

Yarn (4)

Vanna's Choice by Lion Brand Yarn Co., 3½oz/100g skeins, each approx 170yd/155m (acrylic)
• 2 skeins in Sweet Pea #169

Hook

Size J/10 (6mm) crochet hook OR SIZE NEEDED TO OBTAIN GAUGE

Additional

• Stitch markers
• Tapestry needle

Measurements

27"/69 cm x 36"/91cm

Gauge

10 sts and 8 rows to 4"/10cm over hdc
TAKE TIME TO CHECK YOUR GAUGE

Note

Ch-2 does not count as 1 hdc throughout

Stitch Glossary

hdc2tog (hdc 2 sts together) [Yo, insert hook in next st and draw up loop] twice, yo and pull through all 5 loops on hook.

Blanket

Ch 4.

Row 1 (RS) Hdc in 3rd ch from hook and in next ch. 2 hdc. Ch 2 (does not count as a st here and throughout), turn.

Row 2 2 hdc in each hdc across. Ch 2, turn—4 hdc.

Row 3 2 hdc in first hdc, hdc in each hdc across to last hdc, 2 hdc in last hdc—6 hdc.

Jack Deutsch

Rows 4–33 Rep Row 3—66 hdc after Row 33.

Row 34 Hdc2tog, hdc in each hdc across to last 2 hdc, hdc2tog—64 hdc. Ch 2, turn.

Rows 35–53 Rep Row 34—26 hdc after Row 53.

Shape Hood

Row 1 Hdc2tog across. Ch 2, turn. Place marker at beg and end of completed Row 1—13 sts.

Row 2 Hdc in each hdc across. Ch 2, turn.

Rows 3 & 4 2 hdc in first hdc, hdc in each hdc across to last hdc, 2 hdc in last hdc—17 hdc at end of Row 4. Ch 2, turn.

Row 5 Rep Row 2.

Rows 6–9 Rep Rows 2 & 3 twice—21 hdc at end of Row 9.

Rows 10–13 Rep Row 2.

Row 14 Hdc2tog, hdc in each hdc across to last 2 hdc, hdc2tog—19 hdc. Ch 2, turn.

Row 15 Rep Row 2.

Rows 16–18 Rep Row 14—13 hdc at end of Row 18.

Rows 19 & 20 Hdc2tog twice, hdc in each hdc across to last 4 hdc, hdc2tog twice—5 hdc after Row 20.
Fasten off.

Finishing

Edging

With RS facing, join yarn with sl st at 1st marker on hood, ch 2, work (hdc, hdc2tog) evenly spaced around edge of hood to second hood marker to shape the hood edge, then work hdc evenly spaced around remaining outside edge of Blanket, working 3 hdc in each corner; join rnd with sl st in top of beg-ch. Fasten off.
Weave in ends.